DATE DUE

DATE DUE			
MAY 9 1984			
DEC 6 1985			
MAY 13 1986			
GAYLORD			PRINTED IN U.S.A.

BERMUDA PETREL

THE BIRD THAT WOULD NOT DIE

Francine Jacobs

illustrations by Ted Lewin

William Morrow and Company
New York 1981

Library of Congress Cataloging in Publication Data

Jacobs, Francine.
Bermuda petrel.
Summary: Discusses the Bermuda petrel, a bird that nests only in Bermuda, and how it was saved from extinction.
1. Bermuda petrel—Juvenile literature. [1. Bermuda petrel]
I. Lewin, Ted. II. Title
QL696.P665J32   639.9'7842   80-20466
ISBN 0-688-00240-4   ISBN 0-688-00244-7 (lib. bdg.)

Acknowledgment

The author wishes to thank David B. Wingate,
Bermuda Government Conservation Officer,
for reading and checking the manuscript of this book.

For Dot and Don Corwin

Out in the vast Atlantic Ocean, almost 600 miles from the North American shore, a chain of small islands shaped like a fishhook rises from emerald-green waters. It is Bermuda. Although only about twenty square miles of land, these islands are a resting place for birds migrating great distances over the sea. Among these birds there is one that has nested here for over half a million years. It is the cahow (pronounced ka-*how*), or Bermuda petrel.

For centuries, the cahow has been an endangered

bird. The story of its extraordinary struggle to live is an example of the threat faced by many animals that make their home in only one place. Its story is special for another reason too. It shows how people who care about wildlife can affect the fate of an endangered creature.

Petrels are a large group of ocean birds. There are some seventy kinds, and they are found throughout the world, most in warm climates. Petrels spend their life at sea and come ashore only to breed. The cahow is a petrel that nests nowhere else on earth but Bermuda.

Small seabirds about the size of pigeons, cahows are gray and black on top and white on their breast. For their size, their wings are long; outstretched they span thirty-five inches from tip to tip. Those wings take the cahows far out to sea from June to October. Scientists believe they gather over the western edge of the Gulf Stream northwest of Bermuda. But no one has ever seen cahows at sea. Their small size, coloring, and habit of flying low over the waves probably help to hide them. Also, there are so few cahows that they become very scattered over such a vast area. Nevertheless, they are out there feeding.

They pluck their food, tiny fish and squid, from the ocean with their black, hooked beaks. Two small tube-shaped nostrils atop their beaks are used to expel salt from the seawater the cahows drink.

In late autumn, an instinct calls the sea petrels back to Bermuda. They arrive at their old nesting places at night. There they dig long burrows in the ground. These tunnels may reach fifteen feet in length. Each burrow has a bend, which keeps daylight from reaching the nest at its end. The

cahows always use the same burrow; they clean away the old nest inside and build a new one in its place with twigs and leaves.

Now it is their courtship time. The birds court at night. They prefer dark and even stormy evenings to woo their mates. At such times, they fly forth and hover over the sea, not far from the land, shrieking loudly. These courtship calls are a cry that sounds like *aaw-eeh aa-aaw-eeh keeh-eek-eek eeeek,* and they make a terrible din.

When the birds have mated, they fly back to sea
for about six weeks before returning to Bermuda to
have their young. The female lays one large, white
egg in the nest. The male and female take turns
sitting on the egg for several days at a time. Cahow
eggs develop very slowly; they need from fifty-one to
fifty-three days to hatch. (Pigeons, by comparison,
hatch in just seventeen days.)

It is late winter when the little cahow chick pecks its way out of the shell. The parents fish offshore during the day, and each night take turns feeding bits of partly digested food from their gullet to the hatchling.

The chick stays in the burrow all spring, growing bigger and fatter. By the end of May, the soft gray down that covered it at hatching is just about gone, and it has grown black-and-white flight feathers. The parents leave the chick now and return to sea, where they spend another summer feeding in the North Atlantic Ocean.

There is no one to feed the chick. It lives on fat stored in its own body, but it grows hungry. The fledgling must prepare itself for life quickly if it is to live. Once each night it leaves the underground nest and stretches its wings in the darkness outside the burrow. Every night for a week it comes out and folds and unfolds its wings over and over again. It exercises them vigorously in some safe, sheltered area, like an aircraft warming up and testing all its controls before taking off.

Finally, one evening, the fledgling is ready to leave the burrow for the last time. It cleans its feathers

with its beak. Then it climbs to a high point, faces into the wind, and takes off. Up, up it flies, over Bermuda and then away from the islands out to sea. Not until four or five years later will it return to the breeding grounds on Bermuda to mate and have its young.

The cahow has always lived only on Bermuda and had been nesting there long before people discovered the islands. Bermuda was natural and wild then. Its uplands were wooded with palmetto, cedar trees,

and yellowwoods; ferns and grasses covered the lowlands and marshes, and thickets of crooked mangrove trees edged out into the sea along its shores. No animals, except lizards and other birds, were there. The cahow nested and multiplied on the islands without land enemies that could bother it.

There were probably more than a million cahows on Bermuda when Christopher Columbus sailed from Spain to the New World in 1492. Spanish sailors were the islands' first visitors early in the 1500's, and Bermuda is named for Juan de Bermúdez, a Spanish navigator. The Spaniards brought hogs with them when they came, hoping to raise them on the islands for food. Soon these hogs discovered the cahow burrows. They attacked the tunnels with their strong snouts, rooting out the birds' nests, eating cahows and their eggs. The hogs multiplied very quickly, killing more and more cahows.

So now for the first time the Bermuda petrels had an enemy that could destroy them. Although they had flourished for half a million years, they began to disappear after the arrival of the Spanish hogs. In less

than one hundred years only about one in ten still lived, and they survived only because they found safety on a few offshore islands at the eastern end of Bermuda near Castle Harbor. These islands, protected by coral reefs that Spanish ships found dangerous, became the cahows' only breeding ground and nesting place.

By the year 1600, the reefs had wrecked many a ship. Spanish sailors, whose vessels had foundered on shoals at the east end, told tales of demons who haunted the islands and screamed in the night. Diego Ramirez, the captain of a Spanish galleon driven by a storm into Bermuda waters in 1603, wrote:

The first night that I anchored in the bay, I sent

a small boat to an inlet to look for water, but none was found. At dusk, such a shrieking and din filled the air that fear seized us. Only one variety of bird makes this noise, but the concerted yell is terrible, and standing out from it were individual voices shouting *diselo! diselo!* (tell 'em, tell 'em). One seaman said to me, "What is this devil trying to tell me? Out with it! Let's hear what it is!" I replied, *"A la! These are the devils reported to be about Bermuda."*

When the Spanish sailors discovered that the demons of Bermuda were harmless petrels, they also learned that the birds were attracted by lantern light and were tame. They could be captured easily and were tasty to eat. The sailors, eager for fresh meat, took the birds in great numbers; in one evening alone they clubbed 4,000 cahows. Many cahows

were dried and salted and stored aboard ship, to be enjoyed later at sea after the ship set sail.

In 1609, shipwrecked British settlers also discovered the tasty cahow, but they learned a simple way to capture the birds. They stood on the beach and made a lot of noise, laughing and hollering. The cahows were attracted by these sounds and were so unafraid of people that they settled on the arms and heads of the callers. So many cahows gathered that the men could choose the plumpest of them. They caught twenty dozen cahows in two hours in this way. In the weeks that followed, the Englishmen also found the birds' nests and took their eggs.

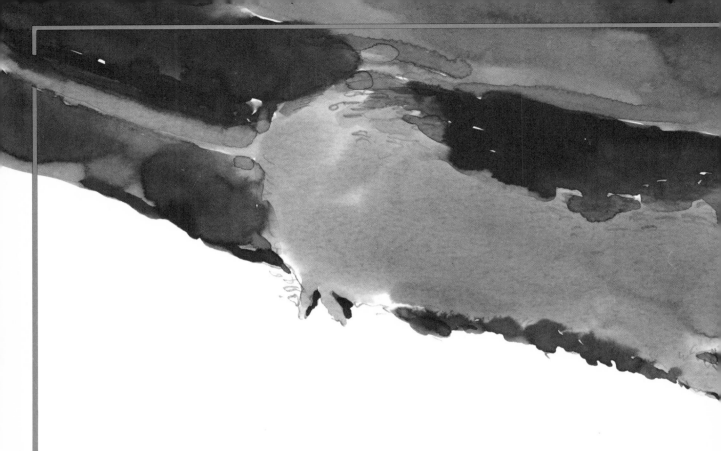

When settlers from England arrived to start a colony on Bermuda, they brought another enemy for the cahows—rats. They swam ashore from a captured Spanish grain ship and ate the birds. They also ate the settlers' food and multiplied. They multiplied so greatly that by 1615 they caused a severe famine in the colony. The settlers were desperate. Then Governor Nathaniel Butler thought of the cahows. He sent 150 men to Cooper's Island, near Castle Harbor, to get them.

The gentle cahows were easy to take, and the hunters became greedy. They killed so many of them that the birds became scarce. The excessive slaughter moved another governor, named Daniel Tucker, to issue a decree forbidding the further killing of cahows only a year or two later. By then, however, the birds were so hard to find that the law seemed almost unnecessary. The cahows had all but disappeared. After 1620, in fact, there is no record that a Bermuda petrel was seen again.

For almost three hundred years cahows were thought to have disappeared forever. Then, on February 22, 1906, Louis L. Mowbray, Director of the Bermuda Aquarium, found a live petrel between some rock crevices on one of the Castle Harbor islands. Mowbray described the bird as a stray New Zealand petrel. He did not think that it could be a cahow as he believed that the bird was extinct. Not until ten years later, in 1916, when R. W. Schufeldt, another naturalist, recognized fossil bones from Bermuda's caves to be from the same kind of petrel did Mowbray realize his error. His bird was a cahow! Bermuda petrels were not extinct after all. Incredibly, some few cahows had managed somehow to nest without anyone observing them. They had survived and kept the species going—though barely.

The reappearance of an animal that was thought to have vanished for all time is almost unheard of. The fossils of thousands of creatures that no longer live fill museums, and none have come back. But the story of the cahow's struggle to survive was far from finished. In the spring of 1935, an American marine biologist named William Beebe was visiting Bermuda to study undersea life. He was working on an island at the entrance to Castle Harbor one evening when he heard bird calls. Aware that cahows had been rediscovered nearby, Beebe thought he might be hearing them. But when he went to look he found a different seabird.

A lighthouse keeper on a nearby island, however, knew of Beebe's interest in birds. So when a bird struck the window of the lighthouse one stormy evening, the keeper wrapped the dead body carefully and had a boy on a bicycle deliver it to Beebe. But Beebe didn't know the bird and sent it to Robert Cushman Murphy at the American Museum of Natural History in New York City for identification. Murphy recognized it as a Bermuda petrel and told Beebe that the precious bird he had been so eager to see had actually passed through his hands.

Still another specimen of the rare cahow was discovered in 1945. It washed ashore on one of the Bermuda islets where an American Army officer, stationed there during the Second World War, found it. As luck would have it, the officer happened to be a naturalist and recognized that the bird might be a Bermuda petrel. The officer, named Fred T. Hall, also came upon the remains of other cahows being eaten by rats. Hall sent the specimens he found on to the Smithsonian Institution in Washington, D.C., and, anxious to help save the birds, he put out rat poison.

This act of kindness toward an endangered creature marked a turning point in the Bermuda petrel's fight to survive. People were now making efforts to help the bird. A Bermudian boy named David Wingate was also on the trail of the cahow by this time. Young Wingate had a special interest in nature; he had grown up studying insects and spiders and observing the stars before his curiosity had turned to birds. By the age of twelve he knew all the wood warblers. He also knew all about the history of the cahow and says that he "spent many a summer holiday exploring for its bones in caves and daydreaming about the possibility of finding it still alive."

In 1950, David, now fifteen, rowed a kayak to the offshore islets to look for a living cahow. The rugged, desolate, little islands have no harbors, and while he searched for a place to land, the sea grew so rough that he was forced to turn back disappointed.

Months later, in 1951, however, David was invited to join an expedition sent by the American Museum to look for and study the mysterious cahow. Together with Doctor Murphy and Louis S. Mowbray, whose father rediscovered the cahow, David Wingate set out by boat for the offshore islands.

Despite rough seas that made landing difficult, the team finally managed to scramble ashore on one of the islands and climb a craggy cliff. At the top, thirty feet above the sea, they found some sparse grass and prickly-pear cacti. They searched the rocky, wind-blown crest and found fresh bird droppings. The droppings were the green-and-white type left by birds like the cahow that feed on squid. Near the droppings there was a hole located between some limestone ledges. Would it lead them to a cahow nest?

The team dug carefully around the hole. It opened into a deep, dark, curving tunnel. Now they used a flashlight to search. After much digging, they were able to reach the bend of the tunnel and shine their light to the end. To their delight, they saw a small bird sitting on a nest there. They inserted a pole with a wire loop, snared the bird, and gently brought it out to them. "By gad, the cahow!" Murphy cried, as he recognized the creature. The researchers examined the bird, took its picture, and recorded their findings before returning it to its nest. The expedition went on to find a total of seven pairs of nesting cahows on two islets. The breeding grounds of the mysterious cahows had been rediscovered.

The cahows had survived on these two and a few other nearby tiny, rocky islets at the eastern end of Bermuda. Their breeding grounds had shrunk to a mere three acres, an area four thousand times smaller than the main islands from which they had been driven. The islets were so bare of soil that the birds were forced to burrow into holes and cracks between the rocky ledges for their nests.

The joy of finding Bermuda petrels alive and nesting, however, was dimmed weeks later when Mowbray revisited the burrows and found four dead

chicks. At first, rats were suspected of killing the
cahow hatchlings. So rat poison and traps were set
out to control the rodents. But then another bird was
discovered to be killing the young cahows. The
villain was the tropic bird, white-tailed with touches
of black and a yellow beak. Because of its two long
tail feathers, Bermudians commonly call this seabird
the longtail.

The longtail, like the cahow, comes to Bermuda
only to breed. It competes with the cahow for the
same nesting ground, arriving around mid-March

when the young cahow chick is newborn. While the cahow adults are away from their nests feeding at sea during the day, the longtails, which court in daytime, kill the cahow chicks and take over the burrows.

Long ago, before the cahows were driven from the main islands of Bermuda onto the offshore islets, there had been ample nesting places for both birds so the longtails did not threaten the cahows' survival. But in recent times, only those cahow chicks lucky enough to live in burrows overlooked by the longtails grew to become adults.

If the Bermuda petrels were to survive and recover their numbers, a way had to be found to keep the longtails from entering the cahow burrows. People first had endangered the little seabird by putting hogs on the islands. Now they had an opportunity to protect the cahow from an enemy.

Richard Pough at the American Museum of Natural History thought of using wire screens to protect the cahow burrows. An American conservationist named Richard Thorsell offered to go to Bermuda the following spring, in 1954, to test the plan. Before dawn, when the adult cahows left their nests for the day, Thorsell placed the screens across the openings of the burrows. At sunset, before the cahows returned, he removed the screens to allow them to reenter.

The screens protected the burrows, but the plan proved to be impractical. The weather and rough seas made the routine of going to the nests twice each day to insert and remove the screens impossible. Some other method of safeguarding the burrows was needed.

Pough had a new idea. A baffle, a small doorway, with a hole just large enough to admit a cahow might be placed over the entrance to the burrow. The baffle would keep the slightly larger longtail out.

Thorsell went to work to develop the baffles. He caught longtails and cahows at the burrows and measured them to help him design the proper opening. Then he experimented. After several tries using baffles with different holes, he found the best size and shape to use. Thorsell recorded his findings in a report and then returned to the United States. A year later he came back to Bermuda at nesting time and installed the baffles. After Thorsell departed,

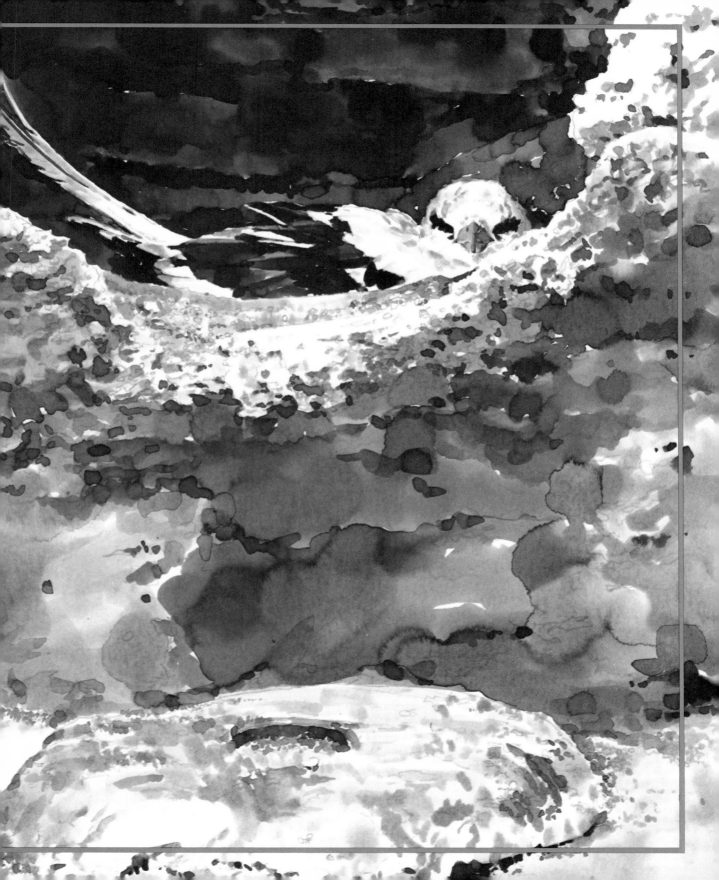

Louis S. Mowbray of Bermuda continued to work on the baffles, changing the size and shape of the holes, hoping to make further improvements.

Then, in 1957, David Wingate, now twenty-two, graduated from college in the United States and returned to Bermuda. Nothing interested Wingate more than the endangered cahows. Soon he set about to do what he could to help them. He found that on three islets the burrows were not protected by baffles at all. On the other islets, Mowbray's baffles weren't working. Wingate was unaware of Thorsell's report with his findings; it had been misplaced somehow. So Wingate had to start all over again, measuring longtails and cahows, repeating Thorsell's work, in order to design the proper baffle.

Wingate camped out on one of the islets almost constantly for six weeks in the spring of 1958. He wrote, "I practically lived with the birds" to get the measurements. His efforts succeeded; he was able to build a doorway that worked. By 1961, every cahow burrow was protected with the new baffle. As a result, more cahow chicks lived. Wingate also built cement burrows with removable lids over the nests for the cahows. When the birds used these man-made burrows, Wingate could observe the cahows and their chicks by lifting the lids.

During 1961, Wingate counted eighteen pairs of nesting cahows that produced twelve chicks. Within a few years, the nesting pairs edged up to a total of twenty-two, but more than half of their eggs were defective. They either did not hatch or produced young that died. After all of Wingate's efforts to save the birds, the cahows were once more near extinction. Like the whooping crane, the California condor, and the osprey, the cahow faced a critical situation.

Wingate and a biologist named Charles Wurster tried to discover what was causing this new problem. They studied eggshells and the organs of dead cahow chicks searching for clues. Wurster found that the chemical DDT used to kill insects was responsible. But how could the cahows have picked up this poison? The islets on which the birds nested had never been sprayed with DDT. The birds must have taken in the chemical at sea where they fed.

Clearly DDT used on land that was hundreds, even thousands, of miles away from Bermuda was reaching the ocean through rivers and being blown by the wind to the sea. Currents carried the poison. Tiny plants floating in the sea absorbed the chemicals, and these plants were eaten by tiny animals that provided food for small fish. The small fish, in turn, were eaten by squids before they were plucked from the sea by cahows.

The Bermuda petrel, like many other innocent creatures, came to be threatened by the use of poisons—long-lasting chemicals—to control pests in forests and on farms great distances from their feeding grounds. Fortunately, the dangers of DDT became known before it was too late for the cahow. The use of DDT and other poisons is much more carefully controlled now.

David Wingate, the cahow's friend and protector, continued to watch over the birds. In 1971, he rescued a hatchling whose parents had not returned to feed it. Wingate kept the chick in a cardboard box and fed it. Later he placed it in a burrow he made for it on one of the islets. When the young bird was strong enough to go to sea, Wingate was there to watch. The little seabird found him, climbed up his

body to the top of his head, and flew from there a short distance. Then it made its way to a ledge and took off.

The cahow population is slowly increasing. There are about one hundred Bermuda petrels now, including thirty nesting pairs, and more young are surviving to become adults and to mate. The cahows' five breeding islets are all protected today. The government of Bermuda set aside two of them for the birds. The other three, which form part of a land lease to the United States for a military base and NASA tracking station, are also maintained as sanctuaries for the birds. No one may visit these islets except in the company of Bermuda's chief con-servation officer. He personally watches over the cahow nests and, like a proud parent at his child's graduation, attends the departure flight of each young cahow. That officer is David Wingate, the boy who cared about birds.

The Bermuda petrel's story is special. It shows that people—even one person—can affect the fate of an endangered creature and save it from extinction.